# Part Time Real Estate Agent Startup

## How I went From Bartending to Be a Successful Realtor

David Newman

Copyright (C) 2016 CSB Academy Publishing Co.

All rights reserved. In accordance with the U.S. Copyright Act of 1976, the scanning, uploading, and electronic sharing of any part of this book without the permission of the publisher is unlawful piracy and theft of the author's intellectual property. If you would like to use material from this book (other than for review purposes), prior written permission must be obtained by contacting the publisher. Thank you for your support of the author's rights.

**CSB Academy Publishing**

CSB Academy Publishing Co.

P. O. Box 966

Semmes, Alabama 36575, USA

Cover designed by

Denise Lowe

First Edition

| | |
|---|---|
| **INTRODUCTION** | 5 |
| **CAN I DO THIS PART TIME?** | 10 |
| **HOW MUCH MONEY CAN I MAKE?** | 12 |
| **BEING YOUR OWN BOSS AND OWNING YOUR OWN BUSINESS** | 15 |
| **50 STATE REQUIREMENTS INCLUDING CANADA** | 18 |
| List of Requirements for All States | 18 |
| **WHAT'S IN THE BASIC COURSE WORK?** | 27 |
| **5 IMPORTANT QUESTIONS EVERYONE ASKS FIRST** | 30 |
| 1. What are the eligibility requirements? | 30 |
| 2. How much money do I need to get started? | 31 |
| 3. How long does it take? | 32 |
| 4. Where and how to take the course? | 33 |
| 5. How to Find a Good Broker? | 36 |
| **9 REAL ESTATE MARKETING, BUSINESS AND TECH TIPS** | 39 |
| 1. Create a Website. | 39 |
| 2. Get on Social Media. | 40 |
| 3. Find Your Style. | 41 |
| 4. Go the Extra Mile. | 41 |
| 5. Ask and Get Reviews. | 42 |
| 6. Be an Active Member of Your Community | 43 |
| 7. Have an Impeccable Business Card | 44 |
| 8. Keep Learning. | 45 |
| 9. Schedule Efficiently | 45 |

## 5 LIFE-SAVING APPS — 47
1. ZILLOW — 47
2. SITEGEIST — 48
3. DICTIONARY OF REAL ESTATE TERMS — 48
4. MORTGAGE CALCULATOR/MORTGAGE CALCULATOR PRO — 49
5. BUFFER. — 50

## HOW TO SET UP YOUR BUSINESS AS A REALTOR ON A BUDGET — 51
## HOW TO BE SUCCESSFUL AS A REALTOR — 53
## SAMPLE PREP TEST: 50 QUESTIONS & ANSWERS — 54
ANSWER KEY: — 74

## CONCLUSION — 76
## IMPORTANT RESOURCES AND LINKS: — 77

# INTRODUCTION

If you are looking for a new career path, I suggest becoming a real estate agent. It is a job that will not only provide you with all the financial benefits you are looking for, but it will also help with building your network and acquiring useful and important skills.

Becoming a real estate agent wasn't as profitable in the past as it is now, mostly due to the recession and the housing crisis. However, for the past five years, a real estate agent's commission has been on the rise again. The commission has been growing at a steady rate, so now would be the perfect time for you to consider it. The average income of a real estate agent is nothing to dismiss, and there is no better moment for you to acquire some of that money for yourself and your family.

My name is David Newman; I was born and raised in Pensacola, Florida. I started bartending back in 2003 and took it as a profession; I was making around $3500 a month, and I was content. But things started to change once I started my family.

I got married in November 2011, and after our son, Jacob was born in March 2013, my wife had to quit her job as Jacob needed some special care due to his chronic asthma attacks. That is about the time when for the first time, I felt the financial crunch, as over the years my income has been on the decline and now with Jacob's health issues I was desperate to find some extra income. I started to have the feeling that things are sinking slowly around me. Some of you may have felt the same way at times in your own life where you feel the wall are closing in around you.

One night at work I was serving this well-dressed older couple some drinks, and we were just talking, I told them my situation, and they were very sympathetic, before leaving the gentleman left me a good tip and his business card told me to call him the next day.

Looking at the card, I noticed he was a realtor broker. I made the call next morning, and he invited me to lunch at his office which was the only a couple of miles from my home. After lunch, he asked me if I would be interested in becoming a real estate agent part time.

He said I would not have to quit my current job either. He explained to me that if I study an hour or so a day for few weeks, I could finish the prelicense course and then take the state exam and if I pass then he can hire me.

He also told me to take the course it would cost me less than $300. I was overwhelmed with information, as I always thought it takes a lot to become a realtor. But he explained the whole process, and I was sold. I needed a way to make some extra money, and I felt in my heart that I could do this.

He showed me how to pick the online school and how to get started. He also told me if I needed his help just to call him and he will help me out. I came home excited and told my wife about the plan. I signed up for the course the same night and started studying.

Long story short, it took me around $250 and three months and one week to finish the course as I was not able to study every day, but only whenever I could. I then took the exam and passed!!! My first call was to my mentor, told him the good news. He was happy for me and told me I should get started the following Monday.

So my journey begins, since my bartending job was only in the evening, I kept both for next nine months. First, six months were a little harder as I only sold three homes and one commercial land and brought home around $11,500 in total but none the extra income was a huge help. But on the 7th month in first two weeks I closed on three homes, and by the end of the month, I closed seven deals! I was on cloud nine as my take home checks totaled $17,217.29

I wanted to quit my bartending job right away, but since I have been there for so long, I just couldn't walk away, I told them to find someone so I can leave, and it took them almost two months to find someone, and finally, I was done with bartending at night.

Fast forward two years, I am still with the same company, I have been one of the top producers for the company for last one year. Since I started, I have helped 4 of my friends including my wife to become a real estate agent now.

I get a request from many others now to help them get into the real estate business, and that is why I wrote this book, I know in my heart if I could do this anyone can. Just follow what I outlined in this book, as long as you put 100% effort and commitment you will be successful, I know this for a fact.

I never graduated college, I am not a professional writer, but I wanted to put this book together as I know it will help a lot of people like myself and not everyone will have a mentor like I did. So my advance apology for any typos or errors you may find in this book.

Just know this, the information I provided in this book are true and correct, and if you follow the steps, you will see success. Good luck!

# CAN I DO THIS PART TIME?

Absolutely, As I just told you I did get started that way and I actually think that becoming a part-time real estate agent is the best way to start.

First of all, it is a great way to learn, without giving up your job or spending all of your savings. I know from experience that doing this part-time is a great way to still learn and have some additional income while not neglecting family life. It is a great job for new mothers, college graduates, and young couples.

You have to realize that a big part of becoming a successful real estate agent is building your client portfolio. By trying to do this full-time from the start, you might be disappointed by how long it takes to close your first sale.

Meanwhile, you are spending and not earning. By doing this part time, you are earning some money, without going through all your savings.

You can start out by getting your license to learn how to better deal with your own property or to help out members of your family. This way, you can sell the property and still get a commission without any fuss. Another advantage of doing this part time is the fact that you can complete the majority of your tasks from home, such as making the necessary phone calls and updating your social media profile for the job.

You only need to step out of the house for showings. But, if you schedule the showings in a way that is convenient for both you and the client, you won't have to ask your significant other to watch the kids for that long, or hire someone to do it. As I emphasized earlier, it's a great career for everyone.

# HOW MUCH MONEY CAN I MAKE?

As you recall, I did very well from the 7th month of starting as a realtor, but most successful real estate agents make a lot more money.

With a lot of hard work and dedication, having a six figure yearly income becomes easy. Surely, if you look at the statistics, you will see the average yearly income of real estate agents being somewhere between forty and sixty thousand USD per year.

That's not much, right? Well, these numbers include all real estate agents, even those who work part time and licensed real estate agents that are currently working in other fields of work, which really decreases the average by a significant amount. If we were to judge only by full time and active agents, the sum exceeds fifty thousand dollars. That's not bad at all. In fact, it depends on how many hours per week you actually work.

Working sixty hours a week will bring you closer to that six-figure number, but you can get there without having to invest that much time.

If you have a good plan, the necessary knowledge and work efficiently, you won't have to worry about your income, and you can pretty much be independent and work for yourself.

I know for a fact that over twenty percent of real estate agents and realtors in the United States make more than one hundred thousand a year.

Being a realtor is basically the same thing as being a real estate agent, with the small difference that you are enrolled in the National Association of Realtors.

Realtors make a little bit more than the average real estate agent, but they also have more rules to follow and are required to do it for a living, meaning full-time.

I have said it in the intro – incomes, sales and other transactions on the real estate market are growing! In the last year alone, most realtors and real estate agents have supplemented their earnings with almost fifty percent. Commercial members are adding international clients to their portfolios and, overall, the more experience you get, the more you will earn.

The time is right for people that want to pursue this career, especially since it means more time for their families – there's an interesting statistic that says that the majority of real estate agents and realtors are actually married people.

# BEING YOUR OWN BOSS AND OWNING YOUR OWN BUSINESS

First of all, keep in mind that, as with any job, the effort you put in will determine the amount of success you are going to have. Being a real estate agent might look like an easy job from the outside, but appearances can often be deceiving. At first, it's possible that you might struggle, but that is what happens until you learn the ropes of working with people. It takes time to build a portfolio of clients.

This is why, at first, real estate agents are working with the help of a broker.

Why should you consider working with a broker before going your own way? There are several advantages such as better marketing and protection within the legal framework.

What's great is that you have a lot of freedom with this job. Even from the start, you can choose whatever broker suits you and your style of working. It all depends on what you are looking for when you start out – if you want credibility, go for a big broker, if you're looking for program flexibility and the ability to handpick the people you work with, a smaller one might suit you better.

After you get some experience and if you think it has what it takes to be successful at this job, you can become your own boss. What does it take to be independent and successful as a real estate agent?

The first and most important thing is patience. Do not get discouraged if you encounter some obstacles along the way, keep working, and I can tell you it will definitely be worth it. After that, learn how to manage your time properly.

Being a real estate agent entails working flexible hours and efficient time management is a step towards success. Last but not least, devote a lot of time to networking. Your network is your path to your career goals.

By being your own boss, you have more than a salary; in fact, there is no limit to what you can actually earn. If you're already your own boss and doing great, you might be overwhelmed by all the work you have to do. At the same time, you don't want to miss any opportunities.

How can you manage? Start your own real estate business and get a team of people that could help you. Having part time real estate agents working for you, or even full-time, depending on the amount of work you have, can be very profitable and marks the start of a new and successful business.

# 50 STATE REQUIREMENTS INCLUDING CANADA

Becoming a real estate agent involves going to real estate school and getting a license. Depending on where you are from, the courses can be short or expand over an extended period of time.

I have included some information in the table below for each one of the fifty states, as well as for Canada. Keep in mind that these requirements may change until you actually want to apply and that there are also many services that offer the possibility to take online courses

## LIST OF REQUIREMENTS FOR ALL STATES

| | |
|---|---|
| Alabama | 60 credits of prelicense courses and a mandatory 30-hour training in the first year |
| Alaska | 30 hours of class and passing the exams |
| Arizona | 90 hours of prelicense classes and |

|  |  |
|---|---|
|  | a good reputation |
| **Arkansas** | 60 hours of classes and a background check |
| **California** | Three classes and a clean record |
| **Colorado** | 162 hours of education, background check and fingerprints |
| **Connecticut** | 60 hours of class for sales people, 120 h and 2 years of experience for broker |
| **Delaware** | 99 hours of class before taking the exam |
| **District of Columbia** | 60 hours of class |
| **Florida** | 63 hours and you have to be a high |

| | |
|---|---|
| | school graduate |
| **Georgia** | 75 hours/10 quarter hours/6 semester hours at a college or university and background check |
| **Hawaii** | Prelicensing course of about 60 hours |
| **Idaho** | 90 hours prelicensing class |
| **Illinois** | 45 hours and at least a high school diploma |
| **Indiana** | Clean record and passing a 54-hour real estate course exam |
| **Iowa** | 36 hours, state exam, background check |
| **Kansas** | 30 hours of class and high school |

|  |  |
|---|---|
|  | diploma |
| **Kentucky** | 96 credit hours, high school diploma, state exam |
| **Louisiana** | 90 hours, high school diploma, background check |
| **Maine** | 55 hours of class, high school diploma and 3 recommendations of good reputation |
| **Maryland** | 60 hours, good reputation |
| **Massachusetts** | 30-hour course |
| **Michigan** | 40 hours of prelicense education |
| **Minnesota** | Three classes state exam |
| **Mississippi** | Resident of the state, 60 hours, |

| | |
|---|---|
| | state exam |
| **Missouri** | 48 hours of class/be a licensed attorney/be granted a one time sitting in an exam |
| **Montana** | At least a sophomore in high school, 60 hours of classes |
| **Nebraska** | High school diploma and 60 hours of prelicensing classes |
| **Nevada** | 90 hours of prelicensing education |
| **New Hampshire** | 40 hours of class |
| **New Jersey** | 75 hours of class and at least a high school diploma |
| **New Mexico** | Resident of the US, 90 hours of |

| | |
|---|---|
| | class |
| **New York** | 75 hours of prelicense classes |
| **North Carolina** | 75 hours of prelicense classes |
| **North Dakota** | 45 hours over a period of one year |
| **Ohio** | High school diploma, clean record, 120 hours of education |
| **Oklahoma** | 90 hours, good reputation |
| **Oregon** | High school diploma, 150 hours of class |
| **Pennsylvania** | 60 hours of prelicense classes/major in real estate |
| **Rhode Island** | 45 credit hours |

| | |
|---|---|
| **South Carolina** | 60 hours prelicense and 30 hours post license and a high school diploma |
| **South Dakota** | 116 hours |
| **Tennessee** | 60 hours |
| **Texas** | 210 hours |
| **Utah** | 120 hours and background check |
| **Vermont** | 40 hours classes |
| **Virginia** | 60 hours, state exam |
| **Washington** | 60 hours |
| **West Virginia** | 90 hours course and high school diploma, background check |
| **Wisconsin** | 72 hours. For apprenticeship 20h/week working with a licensed real |

|  |  |
|---|---|
|  | estate agent and a general knowledge test |
| **Wyoming** | 54 credit hours, state exam |

For Canada, you will need a minimum level of education. Rules can vary according to the region of Canada you are in and the language spoken, but there are classes that you can take in both English and French.

The number of hours required also depends on where and how you chose to attend the class. Background checks or criminal record documents proving that you haven't committed any crime that would disqualify you for the job are sometimes required as well.

Of course, you will have to be an adult to take the prelicensing classes, but in some cases, you can complete your education before turning eighteen and then take the exam once you complete the age requirement.

# WHAT'S IN THE BASIC COURSE WORK?

The basic course structure depends a lot on the state you are in. It can also vary depending on where you take the classes, if it is at a training firm, a college or university and, last but not least, it can depend on how you choose to attend classes: online or in person.

However, all of these types of classes have some basic knowledge that they teach that is common everywhere: the basic principles or real estate and the fundamentals of real estate (or real estate 101, 102, etc.). Everywhere you will go, you will be taught pretty much the same things, but in a different manner and small variations of additional topics which I will talk about later.

At a real estate licensing class you will learn about how to list and sell the property and how to evaluate it. This is the basis of the knowledge required.

You will be provided with additional information based on the state you are in, but you will also learn about real estate at a national level. Then, depending on the nature of the course, you may be taught about the legal framework within the state, the norms and regulations you need to know about real estate. Escrow procedures are also becoming an increasingly useful and popular topic for discussion during a prelicensing course. You will also most likely be taught how to offer efficient counseling for potential clients. Math is an extra topic that many classes do not cover, but you can take it as an optional course for real estate.

Math for real estate basically means you are going to learn about how to calculate a property's real taxes, how to calculate the price/square foot of properties and more importantly, your commissions.

You will learn about marketing, buyer tendencies and more. I suggest you look for the classes you are interested in and asking them for a syllabus or some type of structure. Based on the course structure you can make the right choice for you and learn what you think it will be most useful.

At the exam, you will be tested on your knowledge for both the state and national level and the length of the exam varies by state and on where you've completed your prelicense education. Prelicense education is extremely important – you won't be able to get your real estate agent license without it anywhere.

As for the post-license education, in some places you may be required to attend some classes in order to maintain an active license. In some states, these post-licensing classes are mandatory, and you have to complete them in a certain amount of time. Continuous learning is not a bad thing, especially when it comes to real estate – you can study market trends and a lot of other useful things to help you throughout your career, especially if you are your own boss or planning to start your own real estate business. You can check the table in the previous chapter to see which state require post-license training.

Remember that classes do more than just teach you about real estate. They are a perfect opportunity for networking and learning from real people, from different backgrounds and occupations and their personal experiences. Therefore, I recommend for you to be as active as possible and socialize as much as you can.

# 5 IMPORTANT QUESTIONS EVERYONE ASKS FIRST

## 1. What are the eligibility requirements?

Eligibility requirements vary from state to state. However, there are some common criteria that apply to people looking to become real estate agents. First of all, you have to be of legal age. Some states make that 18 while others 19 or even 21. Then, you have to be a resident of the United States. For some states, you are required to prove that you live in that specific state. Prelicense courses are also mandatory, but their length is established at a state level. In the table I provided in this book you will find information on the minimum hours required for prelicensing education in all 50 states, as well as for Canada. Where you can take these courses also depends on where you are currently located.

After you complete these courses, you have to pass a state-level real estate examination. Try to study and prepare for both the examination and for each class, as there will be plenty of quizzes. The exam and the courses are most often really difficult. In some states, such as Colorado, for instance, the high number of hours of class is finalized with an almost impossibly difficult exam. After you pass, be prepared to attend even more classes. In order to keep your license active, you will need to attend one of these classes at least every three years. Some states even have regulations for mandatory post-licensing classes with a higher number of hours.

Eligibility is also determined, along with all the things mentioned above, by a background test, a clean criminal record, recommendations for a good moral character and more, according to the state you are in. Most often you will be fingerprinted as well, and the background check is a crucial part when it comes to deciding who will actually become a real estate agent.

Once you get past all of that, you will need to take your license to a broker. You will be required to pay some sort of fee, or they will negotiate on taking a fraction of your commission, so it will be difficult for you at first.

If you want to move further and become a realtor, you should know that you need to be a part of several boards and look to enroll in more than one listing service. Additional costs for realtors are the E and O insurances. Overall, prepare to spend a lot for becoming an agent.

## 2. HOW MUCH MONEY DO I NEED TO GET STARTED?

As I said, becoming a real estate agent is not easy, especially from a financial point of view. To get started as a real estate agent, you will need to obtain a license. That means to attend classes that come with a fee. If you want to become a realtor, insurances and board fees will also cost you quite a bit. At first, you will need to partner with an authorized broker, which also means additional expenses and to try to market yourself and get yourself out there. Marketing expenses can be as much as the license, depending on what you have in mind.

You have to save some money for all of these expenses and make some savings for the first months as a real estate agent. Without experience and a solid client portfolio, it will take a while until you can get a commission check from closing a sale. The life of a real estate agent, at first at least, does not imply a monthly check and is less stable.

However, it can be extremely profitable in the long run. It depends a lot on where you are, what classes you take and how much you spend on marketing at first, but I would suggest saving somewhere around two thousand USD. This way, you can get started comfortably and learn the ropes without the pressure of having to earn money.

Of course, this is just a suggestion. You could get started with a lot less, or a lot more – this is up to you. You will have to do a thorough evaluation of your budget before making any decisions and also quite a bit or research on the fees of different prelicense classes, brokers in your area and so on.

### 3. How long does it take?

The period of time necessary for becoming a real estate agent is really not a standard. It varies from individual to individual; it varies according to where they are and many, many other things. I really cannot give you a specific time frame and say "in X weeks you will be a real estate agent." Classes can last anywhere from two weeks to six months because all states have different requirements, different programs. After you pass the exam, the background check or the good character evaluation and so on could last days or weeks. Interviewing brokers and agencies to help you get started might also take a while.

After all, you can't rush to make a decision when the start of your new career is at stake. At this point, you are pretty much a real estate agent, although some people extend that term to the point where you have actually made your first sale. The process usually takes somewhere around six months, but I can't really generalize. The biggest factor here is how long prelicensing school takes in your state and what other criteria you need to fulfill.

### 4. Where and how to take the course?

Again, depending on where you are, you can take the course at a college or university, at a company that specializes in real estate agents training or even with your local Real Estate Commission. In many states, you have the opportunity to take certified courses online.

Online classes have a lot of advantages: scheduling is convenient, you don't have to leave your home, they can cost less and overall there's a lot less pressure on you. For both online and in person classes you'll do all the studying at home. You'll have course material and textbooks available to you just the same, and you probably have the same chance of passing the exam, right? Possibly yes, some online classes are really good, and they work for a lot of people, too.

However, when considering the type of courses you should attend, you should also take into account the advantages of in-person classes. At first, they may seem like a lot more trouble because you have to leave home, maybe leave the kids with someone, figure out transportation and how long it takes to get there and more.

Despite these facts, in person courses give you something a lot more valuable: the opportunity to meet people. First of all, you will be learning from a real professor that will teach you more than just the course material, he will talk from personal experience, give you valuable lessons, provide you with better tips and a more customized experience. You get the chance to ask more questions and figure out more stuff.

Moreover, you get the opportunity to socialize with your classmates. Networking is a huge part of becoming a successful real estate agent, and some of the people you will meet at these courses will go on to become licensed agents or realtors. Needless to say, it's good to have connections. In order to overcome this disadvantage, online classes have set up social media platforms with chats, groups and other similar opportunities for socialization.

You can even organize a study group with some of your colleagues and prepare for the exam together. So, nowadays, both learning and networking are made easy by these two types of classes. It really is up to you to choose whatever fits your style better.

Here are some reputable online schools but remember it is hard to say how much it will cost to attend these schools as it will depend on which state you are in. Best to just get on their website and check the cost for yourself.

1. http://www.360training.com

2. https://www.kapre.com/real-estate-courses

3. https://www.realestateexpress.com/

4. http://careerwebschool.com/real-estate/

for local schools, the best way you can find them is by calling any of your local community colleges or trade schools, and they can direct you to the right place. you can also call the state real estate commission's office and ask them for a list of local schools. but my favorite is just to do a google search for local real estate schools, and you will have a list of them in less than a minute.

## 5. HOW TO FIND A GOOD BROKER?

In my case my broker found me, but that's not something happens to everyone. Finding a good broker to help you get started is of crucial importance for your career as a real estate agent. You can start out on your own, but unless you have already figured out your clients and vendors, and unless you are really knowledgeable about the legalities of a real estate agent's work, I would not recommend it.

A broker or agency will help you with all of the above. Firstly, they will walk you through all the procedures you have to respect on a daily basis, like everything you are allowed to do or say and everything you shouldn't. They offer you legal protection and help you with avoiding mistakes. Afterward, you will get the opportunity to build a network and see how successful real estate agents work.

For finding a good real estate broker, you have two main options. You can go to a well-known broker. This is a good option because, even though they will ask you for an office fee higher than other brokers, you get to learn much faster. By associating yourself with a known broker or agency you also get a good amount of credibility.

Besides, big agencies are generally not interested in receiving a cut of your commission if you make your first sale. Therefore, despite the fact that you have to pay more at first, you are making an investment. This investment will pay off in the long run. The way you can market yourself after working with a successful agency is also greatly improved.

In opposition, a smaller agency will have a much lower fee. However, small agencies will require you to give them a part of your commission when selling a house or another piece of real estate. The experience you get is the same one, but the contacts differ. Just remember that when choosing your broker you are in a position of power. You are interviewing and evaluating the agencies. Try to take your time and ask for as much information as they can give you.

There is no right or wrong answer when it comes to what you should choose; there is only the option that suits you the best. After you get the information you need about the agencies in your area, choose two or three that you like best. Make a list of pros and cons for each of them and compare the lists. In my opinion, this is the best way to find a good broker and make the right decision for you.

Try to get advice from someone with experience and even ask people in your neighborhood about their opinion on different brokers. Did any of them have a positive or negative experience with one of them?

This will help you figure out the image of the broker and what people are going to believe when you associate yourself with a certain brand. You can even ask for advice from family members, after all, they know you best.

Finding a good broker is both important and complicated. With the right amount of planning and analysis, however, you'll see right away which style of work is for you.

# 9 REAL ESTATE MARKETING, BUSINESS AND TECH TIPS

1. **CREATE A WEBSITE.** Nowadays, before making an important purchase, most people turn to online researching. Creating a website is both marketing and a tech tip great for all new real estate agents. When you are creating a website, make sure that it is user-friendly and that it works seamlessly on mobile devices. It will help you look more professional, it will help more people find out about you, you can build your contacts and clients will be impressed if you provide them with useful information. Add real pictures of the houses you are selling, as well as pictures from the area, like the main objectives, how close to subway station it is, other interest points and so on. Let's touch on how

you can get a website on a budget. Let's talk about the cost; you can buy a domain for around $10/year and a hosting account for around $30-$50/year, and you are done.

Nowadays most good hosting companies like Blue Host where I host my sites, are one of the easiest ones to deal with and offer great prices. If you think you want to try this, you first need to find a niche that you want to build a site on, or if you want to start a blog on a passion that you have, then this may be the best time for you to do so. Simply go to https://www.name.com as they are usually the cheapest to buy domains from, then go to Bluehost.com and buy the lowest priced shared hosting account you can buy. Once you do that, you are almost there, time to get help from YouTube, go and search for how to set up a website in 5 minutes and you will be amazed how easy it can be.

2. **GET ON SOCIAL MEDIA.** 84% of Real Estate professionals are now using Social Media, and among all the social media channels 79% professionals are using Facebook as the main channel. On that note, your presence on social media is also extremely important. It gives you a huge amount of exposure, and it helps you to stay in contact with both clients and vendors. You can post

pictures of listed houses, success stories on the field and more. You will be perceived as more professional but, at the same time, more friendly. The best part about being on social media? It's free. Setting up a Facebook page or Instagram account doesn't cost you anything. If you want to reach even more people in your area, you can pay a small amount to promote your page. This way, your page will show up as a recommendation in the newsfeed of your targeted clients.

3. **FIND YOUR STYLE.** Finding a personal style or a niche is extremely valuable. More and more people are drawn towards becoming a real estate agent. The market could soon be overwhelmed by new, ambitious competition or it could even be saturated in a certain area. It is important to distinguish yourself from the competition. Therefore, specialize in something and market yourself accordingly. You can be a specialist in finding houses for single moms, people with pets, eco-friendly houses and more. Try to find your target clients and approach them in that manner. It will make you look more approachable, and it will give you a list of loyal clients.

4. **GO THE EXTRA MILE.** Dedication is what really makes a good real estate agent stand out. Your clients and contact list will grow mostly based on the

people that recommend you further to their friends and family. I can't stress enough how important making a good impression before and after you get a sale is. Before making a sale, it makes sense that you want to appear competent and that you want to close the sale.

So what can you do? If the family has kids and wants you to find them a home, do more than that. Research the nearby schools, both public and private, the fees, how well the kids attending them have performed at tests and other things. If you are dealing with a family that has a dog, give them information about parks in the area, other people with pets, local vets and so on. Do more than just finding the right home for them. They will really appreciate it and will most likely buy through you.

But why should you want to impress a client after they bought from you? Because they will recommend you. If for example, after a young couple bought a house, you surprise them with something small but thoughtful such as a gift card for a local restaurant, they will ecstatic and will give you as an example to everyone they meet. You will then be overwhelmed with requests from their friends!

5. **ASK AND GET REVIEWS.** If you have a website or a social media account, it makes a big

difference if real people are able to post their thoughts on their experience working with you. Give them the opportunity to review you, create a poll or a rating system. This doesn't cost you anything, and you can even choose the reviews that will appear online. Try to get honest reviews. It's good if you have many positive reviews, but don't block reviews from people that say good things and also mentions where you need improvement. You don't want to create the impression that you have all positive reviews and that they are fabricated. Honesty goes a long way in this business. Interacting more with your clients is constructive, as you can learn a lot and grow from each review – you will learn what your best qualities are, what people notice the most about you, what are your strengths and weaknesses, what you can do better. That type of feedback is priceless if you want to become successful.

6. **BE AN ACTIVE MEMBER OF YOUR COMMUNITY.** This is a great tip for everyone, not just real estate agents. It will help you stay in the loop with everything important that is going on in the area. Being involved is a huge image boost, especially since you will be a new real estate agent trying to build a name. Try to be a good neighbor, attend local concerts or other similar events,

volunteer in your free time and, if you can afford it, even sponsor events.

7. **HAVE AN IMPECCABLE BUSINESS CARD.**

While you are out and about socializing, going to showings and more, you will probably hand out business cards. A business card that looks really professional is a huge step in the right direction for you. While we are talking about traditional advertising, it's good to have more than just a business card. Flyers, t-shirts or other types of traditional material are still important. Many people are not as tech-savvy as you. If you do not hand out a business card, they can't find you if they can't go online. Retired couples looking for the perfect home to spend some quiet time and relax will appreciate the extra effort you put in. Traditional media ensures that you reach everyone. Give your card to local business owners; maybe they are interested in starting a partnership with you. Make sure it makes you memorable (but in a good way).

8. **KEEP LEARNING.** Your training doesn't have to end when you get your license. Most states require you to do some post-license training anyway, in order to keep your license. You don't have to stop there. Going to classes and finding a mentor will help you immensely. Moreover, you can join boards, committees, and associations. Learn how to negotiate, take a class on marketing strategies or on the current trends of the real estate market. How committed you are to bettering yourself will reflect on the success you achieve.

9. **SCHEDULE EFFICIENTLY.** As a real estate agent, even though you have a flexible program, you will be asked to schedule showings after work or on weekends. Moreover, some days you will have multiple showings at the same location or a family that you will have to guide to many different houses. Sometimes, it can be hard to keep track; you won't have enough time to prepare or do proper research before a showing. Don't let a hectic schedule get in the way and make you look unprepared. I suggest you find an app or some type of planners that will help you manage your showings more efficiently. Try to separate the time of the day or of the week for

showings and the time you have for making phone calls, updating listings, investigating leads and so on. This way, you will make your work a lot easier and more enjoyable, you will be punctual, and it will help you look professional in any situation.

# 5 LIFE-SAVING APPS

1. **ZILLOW**. Zillow is the perfect platform for you when you are starting out. Although at first it was created as an app on which you can search for property and see photos, the app is now useful for real estate agents more. It has a number of uses. You can look at homes and see pictures and a price, and your search is made easy by diverse search filters, people can use it to calculate the value of their mortgage and also, it activates your GPS to find the best real estate agents in your area. Being a real estate agent with a good score on Zillow will help you find clients with fewer

efforts. You can browse property values, and it is great overall for getting a feel of the market.

2. **SITEGEIST.** This app will help you look really smart in front of your clients and in no time at all. You know when you are going to showings and people want to know everything about the area, the neighbors, and the houses? Maybe you have scheduled a bunch of showings in a day and haven't had time to prepare and do your research properly. Or, maybe you did, but they are asking you something you didn't expect and don't know the answer to. With Sitegeist, you will be able to find out a lot about your surroundings. It depends on what you are looking for. Some examples from the things you can find out are not only interest points nearby but also the average year-round weather, what is the age average of the neighbors, what political inclinations the residents have, how people there commute efficiently and so on. This will definitely give you an advantage over the competition, and it will make you popular with buyers because you will always know the answer to everything.

3. **DICTIONARY OF REAL ESTATE TERMS.** You may laugh about this one, but you don't know when it may come in handy. It's a

great tool that can help you prepare for your state exam, first of all. You will get comprehensive definitions for all the terms you are looking for. After you get your license, it will help you in class, at your post-license training. It can also help you at the office, while researching the real estate market or out on the field. Knowing what everything means will not only enhance your capabilities and your vocabulary, but it will make you look smarter.

4. **MORTGAGE CALCULATOR/MORTGAGE CALCULATOR PRO.** This app will help you with your clients. When people are interested in purchasing a house, they want to know if they will be able to afford it. With this app, you can show that you care about finding them their dream house and lend them a helping hand in need. You will be able to tell them what the price per square foot of the house is, how much it is going to cost them every month but also what options they have for paying it off. Trust me; your clients will be thrilled to know all this information as it will help them make the right decision. Because you've helped them immensely, even if they are not buying a house, they will gladly keep working with

you to find something else. With Mortgage Calculator Pro, you get to see even what type of mortgage to choose. This app will help you keep the clients you've got and will bring you a ton of recommendations.

5. **BUFFER.** Buffer is a free app that is a wonderful marketing tool. It will help you update your social media account with little to no effort. While spending the time you've allocated for promoting yourself, you may find a number of great things to post on your profile. However, posting them all at once might not get each post the deserved attention. With Buffer, you can just schedule your posts. Buffer will automatically spread them out over the span of a couple of days, so problem solved. It will save you a lot of time with managing your profile. For a very small fee, you can have Buffer schedule countless posts on more than ten accounts!

# HOW TO SET UP YOUR BUSINESS AS A REALTOR ON A BUDGET

I have talked earlier about how becoming a realtor implies saving a lot of money beforehand. If you're on a budget, don't worry. There are plenty of ways for you to get all the marketing you need without having to spend all your savings. First of all, getting on social media comes free of charge. If you want to get a professional looking business card, as I advised in the tips section of the book, you totally can, even on a budget.

If you are good with computers, you can design it yourself. Or you can ask a friend or family members that know more about design to create it for you. You just have to print it. The same can be said for flyers, banners, and other marketing tools. Then, you can get free apps for your phone. In the previous chapter, I've recommended a couple of apps that will help you get ahead of the competition with little to no money at all.

As a real estate agent, you'll have to make a lot of phone calls. Worried about the phone bill? Replace traditional phone calls whenever you can with video chats or Internet voice calls. Getting a Voice over IP service is free and all calls and chats are too. You just have to pay the Internet bill to your service provider like you usually do.

Worried about the transportation costs when going to showings? You can do more than just use public transportation or getting a taxi. Commutes can be easy by riding a bike; you can get various cab discounts online, or you can just join a carpooling group, where more people traveling to the same destination post the available information online, and you can join them.

By using a single car not only you will reduce expenses, but you will also do the environment a great service. There are plenty of other ways for you to do great even on a budget too: you can scan your documents on your Smartphone, so you don't have to go back to the office or home many times in a day, you can ask your family or friends to help you with the marketing aspect, you could get some extra money by doing extra work for your neighbors during the weekends or attending local events and more.

# HOW TO BE SUCCESSFUL AS A REALTOR

The very first investment I made after paying for the online school fees was when I went and bought two suits, couple of nice dress shirts, socks, and a nice pair of dress shoes for myself and spent almost $1200. My mentor told me that is one very important investment I had to make first. Looking back I am glad I did. The 2nd big investment I did was after the 7th month, and after bringing home over $17K, I went ahead and bought me a new Chevy Tahoe, yes I did!

To become a successful realtor, you have to know that in this business, appearances matter a lot. For anyone in general, not just for realtors, to become a successful person, you have to act like a successful person.

That means you have to know how to dress. Always put on an appropriate outfit, make sure you have some quality, office clothes in your closet, always keep them clean and perfectly ironed. An unkempt appearance will make clients distrust you more, so make sure to pay special attention to personal hygiene.

Then, when you talk, be well-mannered, friendly and honest. You have to know who your clients are and make them feel comfortable in your presence. Don't talk too much and don't assume you already know what the clients want. Instead, focus on listening more; let them express their wishes about what they want to see.

A successful realtor knows how to market themselves properly. Don't spare any effort to make sure you have the client portfolio that you want. Employ a marketing strategy that entails more than just cold calls.

You can sponsor your profile on social media, pay for ads on different websites and have an e-mail list of customers you send offers to. Don't forget to network. Try to socialize as much as you can, because as a realtor, contacts are the key to success. Give people your business card as often as you think it is appropriate and maintain a good relationship with previous clients, in order to get positive reviews and recommendations.

# SAMPLE PREP TEST: 50 QUESTIONS & ANSWERS

I have included a sample test below, with questions from real state exams for the real estate agent license. This way, you can see what the questions look like, what you should study and more. For each exam, you have a law section and a math section. I will include both sections in the test below, from the Florida Real Estate School:

1.  A buyer purchases a 4-unit commercial building for $150,000 cash. Operating expenses of the building total $30,000 annually. What must the buyer get in monthly rent from each unit in order to achieve a 20% return?

    a.    $5,000

    b.    $2,500

    c.    $1,250

    d.    $125

2.  A small apartment property is estimated to have a potential gross income of $ 25,000. Vacancy and collection losses are expected to average 5 percent over the life of the property. Operating expenses are expected

to average about 30 percent of effective gross income. An overall capitalization rate of 12 percent is derived from market transactions of similar properties. What is the market value?

    a.    $208,333

    b.    $138,542

    c.    $197,917

    d.    $145,833


3. A comparable property sold a year ago for $70,000, but would have sold for about eight percent more today. The appraiser should:

    a.    Adjust the subject price upward by $5,600.

    b.    Adjust the subject price downward by $5,600.

    c.    Adjust the comparable price upward by $5,600.


4. A seller receives $18,000 proceeds from the sale of her home. The mortgage balance was $32,000; she paid a commission of 7%, and her closing costs were 3%. What was the sales price?

    a.    $55,555

    b.    $50,000

    c.    $55,000

d.     $56,000

5.     A comparable property showed the adjusted value of $40,000. The property sold two years ago, and the adjustments indicated a 7% annual appreciation rate. Assuming the appreciation was the only adjustment, how much was the total adjustment?

    a.     Plus $5,063

    b.     Plus $5,404

    c.     Minus $5,063

    d.     Plus $5,600

6.     A home is 10 years old. It has a 50-year life, and a $100,000 reproduction cost. The appraiser assigns physical deterioration of $26,000. Which is probably correct?

    a.     The home has been better maintained than others in the area

    b.     The home probably has a swimming pool or is next to a convenience store.

    c.     The home has been poorly maintained.

    d.     The appraiser is wrong.

7.     A sales associate gets a signed contract from a buyer and sends it to the seller. The seller has agreed to the

terms, and the escrow deposit is safely in the broker's escrow account. The sales associate has a disagreement with his broker and quits. The broker refuses to pay a commission because the sales associate was not in his employ when the contract was actually received and signed. The sales associate should:

    a.    Notify the state

    b.    Sue the seller for his share

    c.    Sue the broker

    d.    Forget it. He is not entitled to a commission

8. A hardware store owner, who is neither a real estate licensee nor a licensed or certified appraiser, was appointed by the court to appraise another hardware store. The person can

    a.    Be compensated for the appraisal.

    b.    Not be compensated for the appraisal unless licensed or certified.

    c.    Apply for a temporary license from the Commission.

    d.    Appraise any hardware store in the state without a license.

9. A buyer gives a sales associate a binder check made out to him. The sales associate should

    a.    Hold the check in the file until the broker returns

and turn it over to him.

    b.    Endorse the check and deposit it in the broker's business account.

    c.    Endorse the check and give it to the broker within one business day.

    d.    Put the check in his personal account, and then write his personal check to the broker.

10.    The F.R.E.C. is composed of

    a.    Four brokers and three lay members.

    b.    Five brokers and two lay members.

    c.    Three brokers, two brokers or sales associates, and two lay members.

    d.    Seven members.

11.    Which is not correct?

    a.    A licensee may be paid a commission only by his employer.

    b.    A licensee may not work for more than one employer.

    c.    A real estate licensee may not appraise a single family residence unless she has been licensed as a state licensed or certified appraiser.

d. A licensee has no grace period for renewing a license, and may not operate while the license is expired.

12. A real estate sales associate is a person who

a. At times may perform any of the services ordinarily performed by a broker.

b. May perform some of the services ordinarily performed by a broker.

c. May not perform any service of real estate for the public for compensation in Florida, unless employed by an owner-employer.

d. May perform any of the services ordinarily performed by a broker provided that the service is under the supervision of the employing broker.

13. The license period is currently

a. 1 year.

b. 2 years.

c. 3 years

d. 4 years.

14. Practicing real estate without a license is a

a. First-degree misdemeanor.

b. Second-degree misdemeanor.

c. First-degree felony.

d. Third-degree felony

15. A sales associate properly licensed with a broker may

a. Open his own branch office with permission from his broker.

b. Manage a branch office.

c. Not manage a branch office.

d. Open his own office

16. Which is correct about a group license?

a. It is issued to sales associates who work for several employers.

b. A broker may have as many as she has offices.

c. It is issued to sales associates who work for several entities with a comm. ownership.

d. It is issued to brokers for each branch office

17. Required brokerage relationship disclosures must be retained by the broker for:

a. Five years.

b. Three years.

c. Two years.

d. One year

18. A sales associate's license has expired. The sales associate is called by a buyer who wants to see property. The sales associate shows the property but does not write a contract until he has renewed his license. The sales associate

a. Is able to do this since the contract was not written during the time of inactivity.

b. Is entitled to receive a commission.

c. Has violated Chapter 475.

d. Is able to discuss real estate with prospective buyers, but may not show or sell it

19. A Kentucky lawyer and a Florida broker joint venture to sell property in Florida for a friend of the Kentucky lawyer. What can the Kentucky lawyer receive?

a. A commission provided he doesn't come to Florida

b. A referral fee if he doesn't come to Florida

c. A commission if he actually performs services in the transaction

d.  No part of the real estate commission

20.  A Fort Walton Beach, real estate broker, is the property manager for several condos on the beach which rent for $1,000 per month. He also manages several (which are rented) that rent for $850 per month. The broker advertises beach front condos (which are unavailable) at a price of $850 and has a good response rate. He is usually able to explain the better quality of the $1,000 per month rentals and rents them quite fast. The broker

a.  Has no problem. He actually manages units which rent for $850 per month.

b.  Has acted in bad faith, but is not guilty of a violation of Florida law.

c.  Has no problem if he can show all customers were satisfied.

d.  Is guilty of fraudulent and misleading advertising

21.  Which of the following is most correct?

a.  All sales associates work for brokers.

b.  All brokers have sales associates.

c.  All brokers are Realtors.

d.  All Realtors must be members of NAR

22. Which of the notices shown below MUST be signed by a buyer or a seller?

   a. Transaction Broker Notice.

   b. Single Agent Notice.

   c. Consent to Transition to Transaction Broker Notice.

   d. Notice of Nonrepresentation


23. A broker decides to go to work for an owner-developer and will be compensated on a salary plus commission basis. Which is correct?

   a. She must be licensed as a sales associate.

   b. She must be licensed as a broker.

   c. She need not be licensed if she confines her sales activity to the one employer.

   d. She must be registered as a broker-sales associate.


24. Which brokerage relationship status requires that a broker discloses known facts that materially affect the value of the residential property?

   a. Any status requires the disclosure.

   b. Single agents

c. Transaction brokers

d. Licensees with no official brokerage relationship

25. A licensed sales associate of a brokerage corporation may

a. Own stock in that corporation.

b. Be an officer of that corporation.

c. Be a director of that corporation.

d. None of the above

26. A single agent broker who wishes to remain loyal to the principal yet is involved in both sides of a transaction

a. Maybe a transaction broker for the other party.

b. May transition to a dual agent with the written approval of both parties.

c. Must work with the other party in a "no official brokerage relationship" role.

d. Are unable to do so if working with the other party in a transaction.

27. An easement created when a person has been using a roadway without permission for over 20 years is called an

a. Easement by prescription.

b. Easement in gross.

c. Easement appurtenant.

d. Easement by necessity

28. All the following are methods of transferring legal title to real property except by

a. A will.

b. A patent.

c. A sales contract.

d. Eminent domain.

29. Which of the following is immediately south of Township 2 South, Range 6 West?

a. Township 2 South, Range 7 West

b. Township 2 South, Range 5 West

c. Township 1 South, Range 6 West

d. Township 3 South, Range 6 West

30. Which of the following is not required on a contract?

a. Offer and acceptance

b. Both parties competent

c. Legal object

d. Execution and two witnesses

31. Title to real property passes to the grantee when the deed is

a. Recorded.

b. Signed and witnessed.

c. Delivered and accepted.

d. Acknowledged.

32. If an owner arrives before the foreclosure sale and pays the entire debt, court costs and legal fees, and interest on the property, he is exercising his

a. Right of stay of homestead foreclosure.

b. Rights of estoppel.

c. Right of redemption.

d. Rights of certiorari

33. Which of the following acts as an insurance agency?

a. Fannie Mae

b. Freddie Mac

c. FHA

d. VA

34. The most common method used by the Federal Reserve Board to control the supply of money is by

a. Urban Development Block Grants (UDAG).

b. Affirmative action.

c. Tandem Plan.

d. Open Market Operations.

35. An example of functional obsolescence is which of the following?

a. Increased traffic flow on the street in front of the house

b. Community recycling plant next door

c. Four bedrooms, one bath house

d. Leaking pipes

36. An appraiser noted a 3 year-old air conditioning system which was operable. He assigned $2,500 depreciation to the system. What type of depreciation is it?

a. Curable physical deterioration

b. Incurable physical deterioration

c. Curable functional obsolescence

d. Incurable functional obsolescence

37. If the capitalization rate increases, the value

a. Increases proportionately.

b. Remains stable.

c. Increases non-proportionately.

d. Decreases.

38. Which is most closely related to the comparable sales approach?

a. Reproduction cost

b. Present value of the income stream

c. Principle of Substitution

d. level annuity capitalization rate

39. Concerning the buyer's attitude and willingness to pay, the lender considers

a. Credit rating.

b. Assets.

c. Income.

d. All of the above.

40. What is not available to the Federal Reserve System in controlling the money supply?

a. Open market operations

b. Adjusting the discount rate

c. Changing the reserve requirement

d. Changing depreciation rules

41. Lien theory means that the mortgage

a. Creates a lien on the property, with the mortgagee having a title.

b. Instrument conveys title to the mortgagee with mortgagor having a lien.

c. Is a lien on the property, but property title is vested with the mortgagor.

d. Is a lien on the property, but property title is vested with the mortgagee.

42. Which of the following expenses is not deducted from effective gross income in calculating net operating income?

a. Depreciation

b. Utilities

c. Advertising

d. Management

43. A seller tells a real estate licensee that he does not want his house shown to ethnic buyers. The sales associate should say

a. "No problem. We probably won't have any buyers like that, anyway."

b. "Will try my best to steer these buyers elsewhere."

c. "I can't handle the sale of your property if you expect me to discriminate."

d. "I'm going to call HUD and report you immediately."

44. Which is not correct?

I. Redlining is not a violation of state and federal laws.

II. "Blockbusting" is a description of the practice of scaring owners into

Selling because of 'undesirable elements' moving into the neighborhood.

III. A sales associate has a direct fiduciary relationship with his seller under

An exclusive right of the sale agreement.

a. I only

b. I and II

c. I, II, and III

d. I and III

45. A prospect enters Broker A's office and requests to be shown houses in neighborhoods with certain racial characteristics. The broker advises the prospect that he will

Show him houses without regard to the racial characteristics of the neighborhood. The prospect is shown houses in certain minority neighborhoods and certain non-minority neighborhoods. The prospect becomes interested in two of the houses, both of which are in minority neighborhoods. If the broker had followed the prospect's initial instructions, which of the following would be correct?

a. He would have violated federal laws but not the Florida real estate license law.

b. He violated Federal and State law and could have been suspended or revoked.

c. He would not have violated any laws; he must follow his principal's instructions.

d. He would not have violated any laws; he must follow his prospect's instructions.

46. A reasonably good balance between supply and demand of apartments is

    a. 5% occupancy.

    b. 90% vacancy.

    c. 95% occupancy.

    d. 87% occupancy.

47. What requires lenders to give a Good-Faith Estimate?

    a. The "Little FTC" consumer protection act.

    b. Regulation Z.

    c. RESPA.

    d. FHLBB consumer protection statutes

48. Which may be deducted for income tax purposes by a homeowner?

    a. Property taxes, insurance, and interest

    b. Insurance, depreciation, and taxes

    c. Depreciation, taxes, and interest

    d. Taxes and interest

49. Usually, local planning commissions are composed of

a. Lay members representing a cross-section of the community.

b. Professionals from each of the local planning authorities.

c. Three county commissioners and two school board members.

d. Local developers and representatives of utilities and banks.

50. Which is correct about Regulation Z?

a. It is published by the Federal National Mortgage Association.

b. It requires the disclosure of pertinent information such as down payment and annual percentage rate if a "triggering" item such as interest rate is advertised.

c. It requires disclosure of an estimate of settlement costs by the lender.

d. All of the above

## ANSWER KEY:

1c 2b 3c 4a 5a 6c 7c 8a 9c 10d

11c 12d 13b 14d 15b 16c 17a 18c 19d 20d

21d 22c 23d 24a 25a 26c 27a 28c 29d 30d

31c 32c 33c 34d 35c 36a 37d 38c 39a 40d

41c 42a 43c 44d 45b 46c 47c 48d 49a 50b

# CONCLUSION

Becoming a real estate agent is a job that implies a lot of effort on your part. You have to always maintain an impeccable appearance. Apart from all the knowledge you have to possess in order to obtain your real estate agent license, you have to learn a great deal of other important things.

You have to become a good listener, to always know you the client, to be outgoing and friendly and to somehow still manage to stay ahead of your competition.

You have to prepare for each showing with the utmost seriousness and provide your client with all the information they require, not only about the property, but the area, neighborhood, city, transportation and more.

However, you will find that it is an extremely rewarding job. It gives you the opportunity to work for yourself, to grow, it offers everyone flexibility and, most of all, you can make a significant amount of money. If your dream is to make six figures each year working for yourself, then it is definitely worth becoming a real estate agent.

# IMPORTANT RESOURCES AND LINKS:

Here is a list and contact information of every regulatory agency/commission of every province and state in Canada and in the US:

https://www.arello.org/index.cfm/resources/regulatory-agencies/#region.1

https://www.arello.org/